This edition first published in 2024 by Red Wheel, an imprint of
Red Wheel/Weiser, LLC
With offices at:
65 Parker Street, Suite 7
Newburyport, MA 01950
www.redwheelweiser.com

ISBN: 978-1-59003-552-8

Printed and bound in China
1010 Printing International Ltd
10 9 8 7 6 5 4 3 2 1

THE ZODIAC GUIDE TO
PISCES

ASTRID CARVEL

Red Wheel

Contents

Introduction

Are you ready to open your mind to the ancient wisdom of the zodiac and explore the possibilities contained within? Astrology is as far-reaching as the night sky itself, an intricate web of stars, constellations, planets, celestial spheres and horizons, mapped out by ancient cultures in millennia gone by in an attempt to make sense of our time on Earth.

This book will equip you with the tools you need to explore more deeply your behaviors, characteristics and connections; to open up the possibilities held in the movement of the planets, and help you to find guidance and comfort when you need it.

Astrology is a voyage of self-discovery, into which you can dip or dive as you wish, taking on a few morsels from the stars or getting stuck in to the complexities held within.

Among these pages you'll find a wealth of insight into the history of the zodiac and the different astrological traditions. You'll learn how to build your own birth chart, what it all means and what you can gain from it.

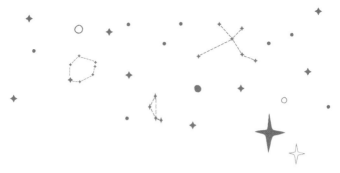

You'll look at how the position of the planets contain meaning, how to decipher your sun, moon and rising signs, and more. You'll look at the houses – the segments of the sky that relate to different aspects of your life – and how to decode their teachings. The patterns created by celestial matter across the houses are decoded here in order for you to easily digest what it all means.

Then you'll move on to the details of your sun sign and how it relates to all areas of your existence, as well as the self-care practices you can benefit from, with ideas and suggestions specific to your sign of the zodiac.

So, what are you waiting for? Turn the page and let the journey begin.

Part 1

WELCOME TO THE ZODIAC

This chapter will take you on a journey through the birth of the zodiac, thousands of years ago, to its relevance in modern times. To understand your sun sign – often referred to as your zodiac or star sign – you might first want to delve into the history and traditions that led to the widely practiced movement that is known today. What moved people to look to the sky for guidance long ago and why do people still do it? Research suggests that today astrology is more popular than ever. It has experienced something of a resurgence, perhaps because the myriad uncertainties of life push people towards the darkness above in search of comfort. The far-reaching knowledge of the stars is yours for the taking – are you ready?

What is astrology?

Before you go any further, it's important to differentiate between astronomy and astrology. **Astronomy** is the scientific study of the universe, including planets, stars, celestial objects and space itself. **Astrology** looks at how the position of the stars and planets at the time of our birth can affect our personality and shape how we live our lives.

While astrology is an interpretation of the position of the planets and stars, it relates closely to human behavior and the influence of celestial bodies on our everyday choices, moods and behavior. Astrologers believe that everything is part of an interconnected reality and that understanding how the ancient symbolism of the stars and planets can relate to events in your own life is a constantly evolving process.

While astrology does not suppose that the planets and stars control you, nor does it predict the future, it does suggest that the celestial sphere is able to create certain conditions and situations that you can learn to use to your advantage. It might take practice, but the potential in the stars is there for the taking.

Horoscopes in magazines and newspapers are just the tip of the iceberg. To find out what makes you tick from an astrological perspective you simply need to know your birth date. From there you can uncover your sun, moon and rising signs, create a birth chart and learn more about yourself. We'll get to those later. The world of astrology is far-reaching and open to all, and can help you to understand your foibles, behaviors and relationships. It can help you decode your past and open your mind to the future.

The first step on your celestial path is a crucial one – it's time to learn about the zodiac.

History of the zodiac

Long before people could travel into space – or even before telescopes allowed us to study worlds beyond ours in more detail – humans gazed up at the night sky to keep track of the time of year and planned their lives around the position of the stars. Many a traveller has looked to the sky to determine which route to take, with ancient sailors putting their trust in the celestial map and using the North Star for guidance. In ancient Egypt farmers were prewarned of the annual Nile flood in July by the rising of Sirius, the Dog Star. The Phoenicians assessed the Sun's position in the heavens when they needed to know which direction to take, and a lunar calendar led by the phases of the moon was drawn up by ancient cultures to keep track of religious events.

While it's something of a mystery when exactly the signs of the zodiac became linked to human characteristics and behaviors, we do know that they originated as a time-measuring device. By mapping out the constellations in a strip of the sky spanning the circumference of the Earth – in which the Sun, Moon and planets moved – and dividing that strip into 12 segments, early astrologers were able to create a calendar of zodiac signs.

The sky is divided into 12 segments and each is occupied by a zodiac sign. Each sign is represented by a constellation that loosely outlines the symbol attached to that sign, and it takes approximately one month for the Sun to travel through each sign's segment. This is the reason that in astrology the signs of the zodiac are known as Sun signs.

While the Ancient Greeks are largely thought to be responsible for devising the Zodiac calendar we are familiar with today, there is evidence of the Babylonians living by a similar set of signs as far back as 1500 BCE.

Why does the zodiac calendar start in March?

The Ancient Greeks believed the first day of spring occurred when the sun appeared in the constellation Aries, marking the beginning of the calendar. It made sense for the year to start with the green shoots emerging after winter, with spring signifying new beginnings.

How it works

There are myriad techniques and applications when it comes to astrology, but the most widely used in the West today is modern or psychological astrology (see page 28).

Before you do anything else, you need to create your birth chart. In the modern age, this can be done quite easily using the internet, however before the technological age those in search of answers in the stars had to search great reams of dusty pages to find the information they needed to compile their trusted chart.

Your birth chart maps out the position of the key stars and planets in the sky on the day you were born. This chart is the basis for every horoscope or reading you might have. An astrologer – or you once you get the hang of it – compares your birth chart with the position of the planets and stars at key moments to understand your motivations. Knowing how the planets behave allows for predictions about an individual's behavior to be gauged in certain situations and at a certain time. None of this is a given, but many find comfort in being granted an insight into their psyche.

Combining the planetary movements with information about your sun or zodiac sign, along with your moon and rising signs (see pages 76–81), as well as your element (see page 24) you can gather more information about what really makes you tick and even understand why certain characteristics of your personality differ from those of other people in your life.

Throughout this book you'll learn about the different aspects of astrology that allow you to access a clearer picture of yourself.

Useful terms

Zodiac – this is a band across the sky through which the Sun, Moon and visible planets move throughout the year. The zodiac is divided into 12 segments according to the constellations that represent the 12 sun signs – Aries, Taurus, Gemini, Cancer, Leo, Virgo, Libra, Scorpio, Sagittarius, Capricorn, Aquarius and Pisces.

Sun sign – this is your sign in the zodiac, relating to when you were born; for example, if you were born on 21 April your sun sign would be Taurus.

Birth chart – a birth chart is a snapshot of the position of the planets on the day you were born.

Planets – in astrology the planets refer to those in the solar system – Mercury, Venus, Mars, Jupiter, Saturn, Neptune and Pluto (despite this being declassified in more recent times). The Sun and Moon are also considered planets in modern astrology.

Houses – 12 segments of the night sky that overlap the signs of the zodiac. Each house reflects a different area of your life.

Elements – each sun sign is assigned one of four elements – fire, water, air or earth.

Moon sign – your moon sign is the sign of the zodiac where the Moon was positioned on the day of your birth.

Rising sign – your rising sign is the sign of the zodiac that was rising (or ascending) on the eastern horizon on the day of your birth.

Retrograde – this refers to an optical illusion that makes it look like the planets are moving backwards, due to their movement through the night sky relative to the Earth.

Midpoint – a midpoint is the measured halfway point between two celestial objects on your chart.

Horoscope – your horoscope is an astrological map of the positions of the Sun, Moon and planets at a given moment in time in relation to your sun, moon and rising signs. This map can be used to help understand past events or hint towards future ones.

Your sun sign

Sun signs are simply another way of referring to star or zodiac signs. With the Earth making one full revolution of the Sun per year, it spends around one month in each of the 12 zodiac signs. Your sun sign is determined by your birth date: whichever sign – be that Aries, Taurus, Gemini, Cancer, Leo, Virgo, Libra, Scorpio, Sagittarius, Capricorn, Aquarius or Pisces – the Sun was transiting through at the time you were born is that which is astrologically assigned to you.

It is impossible to be a "pure" Aries, for example, because all of the other planets would have to be positioned in your sign's segment of the sky at the time of your birth, which due to their orbits and distance from each other could never happen. With the Sun considered the most influential of the celestial objects in your horoscope, your sun sign is believed to be a valuable source from which to learn a great deal about yourself.

However, in order to gain a complete picture of yourself, you must analyse the Sun's influence alongside that of the other planets in your horoscope – the most important being your rising and moon signs. If you don't yet know your signs, you'll learn how to determine these on the following pages. These vital elements of your birth chart (see page 70) help to uncover cosmic insights into your character and inner workings.

How to calculate your sun sign

Working out your sun sign is simple. Check the list below for the sign that falls on your birthday.

Aries	-	21 March–20 April
Taurus	-	21 April–21 May
Gemini	-	22 May–21 June
Cancer	-	22 June–22 July
Leo	-	23 July–23 August
Virgo	-	24 August–22 September
Libra	-	23 September–23 October
Scorpio	-	24 October–22 November
Sagittarius	-	23 November–21 December
Capricorn	-	22 December–20 January
Aquarius	-	21 January–18 February
Pisces	-	19 February–20 March

The signs

ARIES *(21 March–20 April)*

Symbol: Ram
Element: Fire
Ruling planet: Mars

Aries people are brave and headstrong, but can also be childish, impatient and impulsive. They are determined and direct, able to be both straightforward and clear-headed when making decisions. Aries people are natural born leaders and, much like their animal counterpart the ram, they are fiercely independent. They are very passionate thrill-seekers with a zest for life.

TAURUS *(21 April–21 May)*

Symbol: Bull
Element: Earth
Ruling planet: Venus

Taurus people are patient and dependable, persevering to the very end. They show untold loyalty to family and friends, and their quiet strength and determination is an inspiration to others. A Taurus is not a fan of change and does not like being rushed. They long for stability and home comforts. In relationships, Tauruses look for emotional security – they may take their time looking for it, but when they find it, they work hard to hold on to it.

GEMINI *(22 May–21 June)*

Symbol: Twin
Element: Air
Ruling planet: Mercury

Geminis are cheerful and upbeat people, while also being curious and rational. They are good communicators and are incredibly sociable, often keen to engage with anyone and everyone they meet. A Gemini's twin element sees two sides to their personality, and they also have a fickle and superficial nature that they need to work to control. They seek a lively rapport in relationships and have a knack of finding something in common with everyone.

CANCER *(22 June–22 July)*

Symbol: Crab
Element: Water
Ruling planet: the Moon

Cancerians are caring souls who are immensely protective of their friends and loved ones. Much like that of their animal counterpart, the crab, they project a tough, shell-like exterior to conceal their sensitivity. Headstrong and stubborn, it can be difficult to convince a Cancerian to give something up when they have it in their sights. They can also be argumentative, but an overriding kindness runs deep with this sign.

LEO *(23 July–23 August)*

Symbol: Lion
Element: Fire
Ruling planet: the Sun

Leos are attention-seekers who bring energy to those around them. They love nothing more than to have an adoring audience and are proud of their flamboyance. A Leo excels in both creativity and organization, and can be quick to impress this on others whose lives are more chaotic – sometimes without invitation. Leos are often the more dominant in relationships, but bring kindness, warmth and generosity with them.

VIRGO *(24 August–22 September)*

Symbol: Maiden
Element: Earth
Ruling planet: Mercury

Virgos are constantly on the go, busier than all the other signs and in constant pursuit of perfection. Practical, organized and thoughtful people, Virgos are always willing to offer assistance or advice and will help whenever they can. While kind and patient in relationships, a Virgo can also require reassurance to boost their confidence and relax into their situation.

LIBRA *(23 September–23 October)*

Symbol: Scales
Element: Air
Ruling planet: Venus

Libras use their skills of diplomacy to strive for peace and harmony in all areas of their lives. When it comes to decision-making, they can ruminate at length and often seek the advice of others for guidance. These charming individuals tend to shy away from high-pressure situations in order to find a happier balance. A Libra is both romantic and generous when it comes to relationships, however they harbor high expectations in love.

SCORPIO *(24 October–22 November)*

Symbol: Scorpion
Element: Water
Ruling planet: Pluto

Scorpio is one of the more emotional signs of the zodiac, with jealousy an overriding theme that they work hard to contain. However, combined with strong willpower, this can often drive them to reach for their goals. With boundless energy, Scorpios are often high achievers, and their knack for deep, analytical thought pushes them to get to the root of problems. In relationships, when a Scorpio sets their sights on someone, they do all they can to get what they want – and are fiercely loyal.

SAGITTARIUS *(23 November–21 December)*

Symbol: Archer
Element: Fire
Ruling planet: Jupiter

Sagittarians are thrill-seekers who are always up for a challenge and in pursuit of adventure. Their enthusiasm and optimism can be infectious, leading them to be popular among others who often enjoy their company and zest for life. In relationships, Sagittarians don't like to be restricted, and their independent spirit and restlessness can lead them to grow bored easily, needing romantic situations to remain fresh and exciting.

CAPRICORN *(22 December–20 January)*

Symbol: Goat
Element: Earth
Ruling planet: Saturn

Capricorns are realistic and carefully approach situations in a logical manner. Slow and steady wins the race with this sign – with Capricorns quietly moving towards the prize with composure and without haste. A unique sense of humor is a key trait of a Capricorn and, when it comes to relationships, they are both loyal and devoted.

AQUARIUS *(21 January–18 February)*

Symbol: Water-bearer
Element: Air
Ruling planet: Uranus

Aquarians are often glamourous, eccentric people, always friendly and often overly helpful. They are genuinely curious about everyone they meet and will quiz them at great length about their lives, however they tend to shroud their own in mystery. In relationships Aquarians are independent and need their space, which can make it hard to settle down.

PISCES *(19 February–20 March)*

Symbol: Fish
Element: Water
Ruling planet: Neptune

Pisceans are kind people, often going out of their way to be both friendly and charitable. This gentle sign promotes compassion and understanding, and a Pisces is not afraid to wear their heart on their sleeve – opening up and sharing their feelings with those they care for. In relationships Pisceans can be overly affectionate and often keep their emotions close to the surface.

The elements

The 12 sun signs are split into four groups, with each represented by an element. Traditionalists believe these vital elements make up the entire universe. Fire, air, water and earth are regarded as the four basic principles of life, in turn corresponding to four basic principles of the psyche. Knowing our element sign allows us to probe further into the characteristics associated with it.

FIRE

Fire signs: Aries, Leo, Sagittarius

Fire signs are bright and sparky, artistic and passionate. You can expect them to be confident in their independence and never afraid to speak up. Ever the optimists, fire signs make things happen and don't mind the pressure that might come along with it.

AIR

Air signs: Libra, Aquarius, Gemini

Air signs are social creatures, they know how to work the room and offer engaging conversation. While equally witty and entertaining, they are also good listeners and know when to offer a sympathetic ear to others.

WATER

Water signs: Cancer, Scorpio, Pisces

Water signs are in touch with their emotions, and are both empathetic and nurturing to others. Always ready to offer help, they will step up when they are needed. Water signs are imaginative and can be quiet thinkers.

EARTH

Earth signs: Capricorn, Taurus, Virgo

Earth signs are all about the details. While they are practical and grounded, they look to the future and start building for it way ahead of time. Earth signs are down-to-earth people and are often called the "gardeners of the zodiac", in part due to the care and attention they pay their family and friends.

The fifth element

Some Western sources believe in a fifth element known as the *quinta essentia* – or simply, "spirit". This element is frequently overlooked because it describes the soul or spiritual being of someone and stands apart from the other four elements. While some astrological applications take the fifth element into account when analyzing signs, it is not depicted in the horoscope.

Different astrological traditions

Over the centuries, different cultures around the world have developed their own astrological traditions and systems. It's fascinating to see how these differ and how they all came about.

WESTERN

In the West, the most commonly used astrological system is derived from the ancient form of astrology based on the 12 signs of the zodiac. This system spans popular culture in its basic form of sun sign horoscopes focusing on human behavior and motivation, and is led by the 12 constellations attached to the 12 sun signs.

MAYAN

Mayan astrology is based on an ancient and complex calendar known as the Tzolk'in, which consists of 20 day signs and 13 galactic numbers. The 260-day calendar is often used to suggest future events and identify different human characteristics. Instead of elements, the Mayan astrological system uses directions – north, east, south, west – which each carry a different set of meanings and a direction is assigned to each of the 20 day signs.

VEDIC

Vedic - or jyotish - astrology is derived from ancient Indian traditions and is one of the oldest and most-practiced forms of astrology in the East. While the vedic and Western zodiac follow pretty much the same 12 signs, the dates are different - for example, Aries runs from 13 April-14 May, while Taurus sits between 15 May-14 June (as opposed to 21 March-20 April for Aries and 21 April-21 May for Taurus in the Western calendar). This is because it is based on the fixed, observable positions of the related constellations, whereas Western astrology takes into account the shifting of the Earth on its axis over millennia and is instead based on the changeable position of the sun.

CHINESE

This system is based on the lunar cycles and the power of five elements - wood, fire, earth, metal and water. Drawing from ancient Chinese philosophy, and the concept of yin and yang, each year is associated with an animal as well as an element.

Different astrological techniques

There are many different astrological practices, but the ones outlined below are some of the most widely used across the world.

MODERN ASTROLOGY

Also referred to as "psychological astrology", this is the most popular type of astrology in the West and is the technique that will be the focus of this book. It is a practice with many layers, but in simple terms, modern astrology looks at the position of the planets in relation to your birth chart – which is a snapshot of the planets and stars on the day you were born – and uses the information to understand your personality, characteristics and behaviors.

Alan Leo was a respected British astrologer who revived the practice in the late 1800s and early 1900s, following its fall from favor at the end of the 1600s. Leo – who used his sun sign as a pseudonym – is widely referred to as the "father of modern astrology", thanks to the way he helped to move it away from fortune-telling and encouraged people to use it to explore behavior and personality through a psychological lens.

HORARY

The Horary astrology technique is rooted in ancient Hellenistic traditions and seeks to answer a question by creating a horoscope for the moment the question is asked. The astrologer will generally receive a simple "yes" or "no" answer to the question being posed.

MUNDANE

Mundane astrology studies the effect of the planets on groups of people, places and countries. This branch of astrology focuses on significant events throughout history and looks to understand it through the creation of a birth chart for that moment in time. A horoscope can then be created for that event to explain how people might react to or cope with such an event.

ELECTIVE

Elective astrology looks at the optimal time for an event to occur, based on the position of the planets. An astrologer might advise you to get married at a time when Venus – the planet of love and harmony – is aligned with the planet's position on your own birth chart, for example.

RELATIONSHIP

This branch of astrology looks at how compatible two individuals are likely to be in love. An astrologer will study the birth charts of the two individuals to see how well they will get along. There are two ways of doing this. The first is synastry, which compares the two birth charts side by side; and the second is composite, which involves calculating the midpoints of the planets on each person's birth chart to create a new chart for the pairing, which is then interpreted afresh.

TRADITIONAL

Until the twentieth century and the introduction of modern astrology, most branches of the practice were considered "traditional". This form is all about prediction and only uses the seven "planets" we can see with the naked eye to do so, namely the Sun, Moon, Mercury, Venus, Mars, Jupiter and Saturn.

LOCATIONAL

Locational astrology looks at a birth chart to determine where the bearer should exist or spend time. According to the position of certain planets in relation to the subject's own, they can advise where they should live or go on holiday. If someone wanted to know where they were likely to have the most successful holiday, for example, an astrologer might look at the position of Venus (representing enjoyment) and Jupiter (long-distance travel) in order to deduce the ideal location. This is also known as "astro-mapping".

MEDICAL

Medical astrology is all about the health of a person, whereby an astrologer uses an individual's birth chart to discover the cause of any health issues they may have. The health problem, cures and area or areas of the body in which it occurs all correspond to specific planetary positions.

Science fiction?

Modern astrology is more popular than ever, with younger generations increasingly adopting the practice in an attempt to understand their own lives. And they hold it in high esteem: a National Science Foundation poll conducted in recent years found that more than half of millennials believe astrology to be a science.

What astrology can do for you

Astrology does not predict your future or describe your personality in certain terms; instead it describes the potential for particular characteristics or events to come to light. Astrology can help you know what you are capable of as a human being, and when to take advantage of challenging or opportunistic times. Astrology does not negate your own free will – you are not controlled by the planets – but the planets do create certain atmospheres and conditions that you can learn to use to your advantage.

When you understand why you act in a certain way or acknowledge your fears and desires, you feel more at ease with yourself and your world. When you know yourself better you act with conscious awareness of what you're doing and why.

ASTROLOGY IS A
LANGUAGE. IF YOU
UNDERSTAND THIS
LANGUAGE, THE SKY
SPEAKS TO YOU.

DANE RUDHYAR

Part 2

MEET PISCES

The twelfth and final sign of the zodiac, Pisces is a kind and gentle soul, open and devoted to those they hold dear. Sometimes you prefer the dream to the reality – but then, don't we all? You are hugely creative, with a brilliant imagination, but are not a fan of pressured situations and tend to retreat when they arise. You are quite selfless in the way you assist others and are very likely to be involved in several charitable causes. Over the following pages we'll take a more detailed look at what really makes you tick in all areas of life, from career to wealth, love and romance, relationships with friends and family, health and well-being, and compatible signs. We'll find out what the planets mean to you, as well as your strengths and challenges.

Factfile: Pisces

DATES: 19 February–20 March

REPRESENTATION: Fish

SYMBOL: ♓

CHARACTER TRAITS: Dreamy, psychic, gentle

BODY PART: Feet

ELEMENT: Water

RULING PLANET: Neptune

COLOR: Light green

BIRTHSTONE: Amethyst (February), aquamarine (March)

ASSOCIATED CRYSTALS: Clear quartz, carnelian, chrysocolla

CHAKRA: Sacral

TRIVIA

✦ Pisces is the twelfth and final sign of the zodiac, after Aquarius and before it all starts again with Aries. Pisces is the last of the water signs, the others being Cancer and Scorpio.

✦ The word "Pisces" means "fish" (plural) in Latin and the symbol for the constellation is two fish swimming in opposite directions.

✦ In Greek mythology, the fish are said to represent the goddess Aphrodite and her son Eros.

✦ Pisces lies on the vernal equinox, which is the point at which the sun crosses the celestial equator into the northern hemisphere every year around 20 March. This used to be located in Aries, but has shifted due to the Earth's wobble on its axis.

✦ None of Pisces' stars are overly bright, meaning it can be tricky to spot with the naked eye. It can be seen most clearly in the northern hemisphere in early autumn.

✦ Pisces' brightest star is known by several names – Eta Piscium, Alpherg and Kullat Nunu. This giant star is located 294 light years from Earth and is said to have 316 times the luminosity of the sun.

The history of Pisces

Pisces is deeply rooted in Greek mythology and is associated with the story of the goddess Aphrodite and her son Eros.

The myth goes that Aphrodite and Eros were walking along the banks of the Euphrates river, when they were accosted by the fearsome giant Typhon. This beast had the body of a man, wings and a bottom half consisting of vipers that hissed and snapped as he moved.

Typhon was sent down from Mount Olympus by his mother – Gaia, who was Mother Earth – to declare war on all the Greek gods. Typhon caused untold destruction, whipping up storms and breathing fire at all in his wake.

Zeus saw that Aphrodite and Eros were in trouble and swiftly intervened. He turned the pair into fish and tied them to one another, allowing them to jump into the river and swim away from Typhon at great speed, all the while remaining bound together.

The goddess Athena is said to have placed them in the sky as the constellation Pisces, in honor of their bravery in the face of the terrifying Typhon.

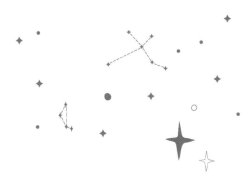

Pisces:
what the planets tell us

One of the most important strands of astrology is what the planets can tell us when they are transitioning through your sun sign. You can find planetary transition predictions on various websites including this one: astrosage.com/transits. Note: as outer and therefore slower-moving planets, Uranus, Neptune and Pluto take hundreds of years to move through all 12 signs of the zodiac! Therefore what they can tell us is far broader and less personal.

The Sun: purpose – You are selfless in your pursuit of helping others and are proud of your dedication to worthy causes.

The Moon: instinct – It takes time for you to assess your feelings in relation to those of others and time alone is vital to mull things over.

Mercury: communication – You learn best when going at your own pace and process information in an imaginative way.

Venus: love – You are a romantic soul and have the ability to inject a sense of magic into a relationship.

Mars: action – When things get tough, you want nothing more than to run and hide – but if others need your help, you stick around.

Jupiter: opportunity – You take any opportunity to get away from it all and escape to somewhere new or into deep relaxation.

Saturn: authority – You sometimes struggle with boundaries, but with some guidance will work out how to deal with these.

Uranus: change – Uranus represents sudden change and innovation, as well as the advancing of science and technology.

Neptune: imagination – As well as intuition, glamour and enchantment, Neptune moves us to ask ourselves important questions in the quest for another path.

Pluto: power – Pluto is about the bigger picture and not worrying about the small stuff. Due to its incredibly slow orbit, it can take between 12 and 30 years for Pluto to move through one sign – and a whopping 248 years to transition through the whole zodiac. This is why Pluto is known as "the generational planet", with whole generations finding Pluto on their birth chart.

2060 Chiron

Some branches of astrology also include 2060 Chiron, a minor planet in the outer solar system orbiting the sun between Saturn and Uranus. Discovered in 1977, it suggests that self-assurance will promote healing as you look to find independence from your situation.

Pisces: personality traits and characteristics

Pisces is traditionally known as the poet of the zodiac, thanks to your vivid imagination and the way you view the world. You are likely to be spiritual and can be quite visionary, seeing the bigger picture and cutting through the noise in a way that others cannot. However, sometimes your imagination runs away from you and you prefer a dream world to reality.

You are kind and gentle, emotionally open and devoted to charitable causes. You're a real helper and people rely on you when they need support.

Compassionate and understanding, you have been known to shift focus from your own life to the lives of those who need your help – so much so that you detach from yourself and your own needs.

You don't like pressured situations and are a true escapist, preferring to meditate, watch endless TV or go on a trip if it means you can forget about what's going on in the here and now.

You struggle with commitment and willpower, but with the right support can triumph over these things. Your true strengths are your sweet nature and your capacity for quite brilliant creativity – and when you find the drive to see a project through to the finish you can come up with something truly wonderful.

Pisces: strengths and challenges

STRENGTHS

+ Your imagination is like no other in the zodiac. Your capacity for creative genius can be quite astonishing and if you let your true talents shine through you can achieve greatness in this field.

+ You are truly selfless in your pursuit of helping others. You champion worthy causes close to your heart and are willing to fight against the injustices in the world to make a difference to those who need it.

CHALLENGES

+ You are not the most proactive sign in the zodiac and can be prone to inaction. Sometimes you need a boost to get you moving, which can be a challenge, but when you do find the fire to keep going you do brilliant things.

+ Your organizational skills leave a lot to be desired and this extends to all areas of life. Try using simple tools like online calendars and apps to keep things in order and seek professional advice if things get out of hand.

Pisces: interests, likes and dislikes

INTERESTS

Your creative talents mean you are most at home when you are making art – whether painting, sculpting, textiles, digital or installation; these things really get your heart racing.

Making useful things with your hands is another passion of yours. Knitting, crochet and sewing your own clothes brings you joy, as does creating bits of furniture or garden pieces from wood or reclaimed items.

LIKES

You love to make your home beautiful and unique, whether through painting murals on the walls or choosing unusual color schemes.

You get immense satisfaction from teaching others how to be creative too and sharing your talents with them. You're the first to offer a skill swap or to show someone how easy it is to create things for themselves.

DISLIKES

You are not a fan of long-term projects and tend to start many more than you finish. Try getting to the end of something before moving on to the next and enjoy the satisfaction this brings you.

You don't like to be under pressure and can retreat from the world when you find yourself in a stressful situation. Try talking the situation through with friends or family and taking things one step at a time.

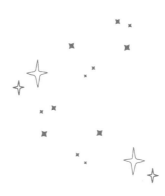

Pisces: communication style

Pisceans are friendly souls, always happy to talk to anyone and for this reason you get invited to a lot of dinner parties and get-togethers. You don't shy away from chit-chat with strangers at the bus stop and are always charming when engaged by other people.

You are emotionally open and don't hold back when it comes to sharing details about your life with other people. It has been suggested that you can be an oversharer and should keep some things to yourself.

While those in your inner circle consider you trustworthy, sometimes your wild imagination means you can embellish the truth and some people are unsure about what to believe.

You have a kind and gentle nature, but there is a fiery temper lurking below the surface that will rear its head if you are pushed too hard. The fire lies fairly deep within you and it takes a lot for your eyes to blaze with fury, but when that fury is unleashed all hell breaks loose.

You have an intuitive understanding of others that some people find almost spooky and bordering on psychic ability.

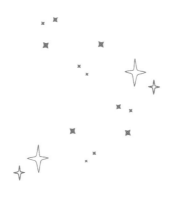

Pisces: compatibility with other signs

Remember this is not hard and fast – the zodiac moves in mysterious ways and just because your sign might appear incompatible with that of someone you are close to doesn't mean a friendship or more is off the table. As always, the zodiac is just a guide.

Aries – Pisces finds safety and comfort in Aries, while Aries admires Pisces' ability to connect with others.

Taurus – These two are a huge inspiration to each other and friendship develops easily, before turning into something more.

Gemini – Despite often having little in common, Pisces and Gemini feel right at home with each other.

Cancer – Pisces and Cancer are easy company for each other and understand what the other needs from the relationship.

Leo – These two open up to each other in an enviable way and explore their feelings side by side.

Virgo – While very different, both of these signs share a deep commitment to helping others.

Libra – As indecisive as each other, Pisces and Libra have a special connection and understanding of each other.

Scorpio – These two open up different worlds and inspire each other through new experiences.

Sagittarius – Passions run high between these two and they are a great source of encouragement for each other.

Capricorn – Communication is strong between Pisces and Capricorn, and they share a unique sense of humor.

Aquarius – These two signs are both very creative, but need to keep talking about their feelings.

Pisces – Double Pisces can see a slow start to any relationship, but when they finally get together the bond is strong.

Pisces: relationships – friends and family

While sociable, Pisceans are not likely to invite any but their closest family and confidants into their home.

It might be a bit of a disorganized jumble, but your home is your sanctuary – where you like to retreat to when things get too much – and you'd rather keep it for yourself than share it with others.

The thought of having someone outstay their welcome when all you want to do is escape to bed is a bit too much for you to bear.

You are a caring and loving individual and make sure that those who are important to you know their value to your life. You have a lot of love to give and are keen to understand them. Just be mindful that not everyone thinks the same way as you do about every aspect of life and it's important to acknowledge our differences.

As a parent you are great at encouraging your children's interests and helping them to fulfill their potential.

You are loving and nurturing, keen to help grow your offspring's confidence in all areas of life and introduce them to an array of hobbies.

Be careful to recognize your child's own interests and personality traits rather than forcing your own on to them.

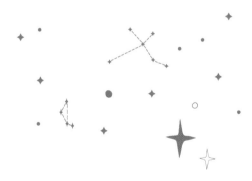

Pisces:
love and sex

In relationships, Pisceans wear their hearts on their sleeves and are incredibly tactile. You can be overly affectionate, which your partner might find over-whelming. Read the situation and take a step back if it feels like you're coming on too strong.

You are kind and caring with those you love and greatly sensitive to the needs of your partner, which they should appreciate. You nurture them with the encouragement they need and are supportive of their decisions and choices.

Sometimes you can find yourself in a situation where you feel your partner can do no wrong, which can lead to imbalance in the relationship. Your chosen partner may well be wonderful, but we are all human and all have our flaws.

You keep your emotions close to the surface and can become easily upset about matters the other might consider trivial. Make sure you keep communication lines open and flowing in order to truly understand what the other needs in the situation.

You have a very romantic and traditional view of sex and are best suited to someone who shares this with you. However, don't be afraid to gently experiment with your partner if you feel comfortable doing so.

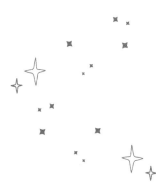

Pisces:
career and success

Pisceans are not hugely ambitious, unlike some of the other signs, or the most proactive.

You can be prone to inaction and sometimes need encouragement to get moving and make things happen. When you do have a fire lit underneath you, you can be a wonderfully creative thinker and come up with big, innovative ideas that are both unique and hugely imaginative.

Every boardroom needs a Piscean to freshen things up and give people a new perspective – the catch is, however, that you're not usually the boardroom type so are unlikely to be lurking there. You're more like a consultant, greatly preferring to carve your own path and work for yourself.

You need a career that is both varied and interesting, so self-employment suits you to a tee and it's likely you have multiple jobs at the same time.

Working for yourself also takes the pressure off, which is important to you. You take on as much work as you can handle and take a break when you need to.

As well as the creative industries, you are well-suited to jobs in science, research and the caring professions, particularly counseling, nursing and social care.

Pisces:
money and prosperity

Pisceans' disorganization can extend to their finances, so it's important to keep an eye on this area of your life.

Whenever a big purchasing decision arises, you would do well to seek financial advice and do more research than you think you need to. Cover all bases and get the facts before making your choices and things will go well.

You are one of the most generous signs in the zodiac and your keenness to help others in need can extend to using what money you have to come to their aid. This is admirable and kind, but be careful not to give away more than you can afford.

Unfortunately, your financial generosity can mean you are sometimes relied on by those close to you as good for a loan when they are short of cash. Just make sure you feel financially secure enough in yourself before you put your hand in your pocket.

WITHOUT ASTROLOGY
MAN TREADS, AS IT WERE,
IN THE DIM TWILIGHT
OF IGNORANCE.

LUKE DENNIS BROUGHTON

Pisces: health and well-being

It's important for Pisceans to switch off and practice some self-care when needed – even when you don't think it is.

Incorporating a regular yoga class into your schedule can work wonders for your mind and body, giving you space to breathe.

If you can fit it in, daily guided meditation for five or ten minutes will do you the world of good. It's important to look after your busy brain and ensure you don't burn out.

Regular outdoor exercise can also be a tonic for you. Embrace outdoor pursuits that are good for the soul – get out in nature and go for a walk or a hike.

You could even try some forest bathing – the Japanese have embraced this form of ecotherapy, which involves walking or immersing yourself in nature and consciously connecting with your surroundings.

The benefits to your physical and mental health are manifold.

Wild or cold-water swimming is another way to use the benefits of nature to your advantage. Many fans of wild swimming claim to feel energized for the rest of the day following a dip, and the benefits of cold-water therapy are held in high esteem by many – look into the Wim Hof method if you want to know more.

Part 3

YOUR HOROSCOPE AND YOU

This is where you start putting your knowledge into practice – it's time to build a birth chart. Over the following pages you'll learn how to do that and most importantly how to decode it. It might look complicated at first glance, but don't worry – all the elements and information you need to understand your chart are here in this chapter. We'll guide you through, step by step, and help you to make sense of it all. From your moon and rising signs, to the meanings hidden in the planets and houses, the mysteries of the night sky are about to be revealed.

Using astrology for divination and guidance

By mapping out a birth chart and discovering the position of the planets and zodiac signs in the sky and which particular astrological house they were occupying when you were born, you can gain a deeper insight into yourself. Armed with this knowledge you can learn more about who you are, your motivations and what makes you tick. You could also gain a greater picture of who you might become, what prospects lie ahead and how you can potentially work them to your advantage.

Whether you feel misunderstood or simply want some clarity, you might find solace in the sky. When big decisions loom, you might look to astrology for comfort and reassurance. While astrology does not spell out the answers, it will give you much to ruminate on and relate to. With the houses covering so many aspects of your life, and the planets and zodiac signs looking to your personality, there's a lot of coverage up there!

In the following pages you will learn how to cast your birth chart (this is much easier than it used to be, thanks to modern technology and the internet) and learn what all the segments and symbols mean; how to work out your moon and rising signs; and gain greater knowledge about the planets and houses, their influence on your life and how to interpret their meaning.

Dos and don'ts when interpreting the stars

DO

✦ Remember astrology is all about guidance

✦ Sleep on it before making any big decisions

✦ Seek a reading from an experienced astrologer if you are worried or need clarity on your reading

DON'T

✦ Take things too literally – these are interpretations, presented for you to find meaning in them in relation to your life

✦ Rush yourself – go at your own pace and all will become clear

✦ Obsess over your results – tomorrow is another day and things could change

**A CHILD IS BORN
ON THAT DAY AND AT
THAT HOUR WHEN
THE CELESTIAL RAYS
ARE IN MATHEMATICAL
HARMONY WITH THEIR
INDIVIDUAL KARMA.**

SRI YUKTESWAR

How to create your own birth chart

To create your birth chart you simply need to know the day on which you were born and the location. It is, however, vital that you know exactly what time you were born on that day. If you don't know, ask relatives, consult medical records or dig out your baby book – if you have one – because it is impossible to create an accurate birth chart without this information.

Sometimes referred to as a "natal chart", your birth chart is essentially a snapshot of the position of the planets and stars in the sky at the exact moment of your arrival on Earth. It's a wholly unique arrangement, never to be repeated, and can bring you so many valuable insights in your quest to better understand yourself.

Creating a birth chart used to be a painstaking process, but thanks to the power of the internet you can now be presented with yours in minutes. Try astro.com and opt for one of their free birth charts, from simple to complex; I say "simple" – even the simplest birth chart will look a bit indecipherable the first time you see one, but you'll soon get the hang of it.

TimePassages is a very user-friendly paid-for app where you can create a birth chart and read daily horoscopes based on your personal information and astrological transits – as well as compare your chart with a friend or partner's – should you want to delve a little deeper.

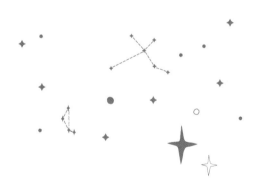

An example birth chart

Symbols

ARIES   TAURUS   GEMINI   CANCER

LEO   VIRGO   LIBRA   SCORPIO

SAGITTARIUS   CAPRICORN   AQUARIUS   PISCES

PLANET SYMBOLS

SUN   MOON

MERCURY   VENUS   MARS   JUPITER   SATURN

URANUS   NEPTUNE   PLUTO

How to decipher your birth chart

It's a good idea to keep an open mind when reviewing your birth chart. Be flexible, be imaginative and be prepared to take on the challenges it presents. Explore the potential it offers and be open to suggestions you might not previously have expected.

We've talked about the signs of the zodiac already, and in the following pages we'll look at the planets and the houses. These are the most important elements of the birth chart.

You will find around the outer wheel the 12 signs of the zodiac, while the inner 12 segments that overlap these are the houses.

The line across the middle is the horizon, with "AC" for ascendant, or rising sign, and "DC" for descendant. Look to the vertical line and "MC" is for midheaven and "IC" for *imum coeli* (loosely translating as "bottom of the sky").

Now it's time to work out what it all means. Follow the instructions on the following pages to find out how.

THE PLANETS

Look at the planets one by one and where they are placed on the chart. The simplest way to explain these is that the planets tell you "what", the sign it is transitioning through tells you "how" and "why", and the house the planet appears in represents the area of life to which this is relevant. As the twelfth sign of the zodiac Pisces rules the twelfth house. This means that this particular house is associated with Pisces energy. Looking at the example birth chart on page 70, the Moon is transitioning through Sagittarius and the twelfth house. From this we can take the Moon to signify compassion, and Sagittarius to represent escape – perhaps alluding to a caring role from which you could do with a break – in the twelfth house, which symbolizes sacrifice.

PLANET CLUSTERS

Clusters of planets on the chart can also be revealing. The upper hemisphere of the chart represents your public life, while the lower hemisphere represents your private life. The west half represents freedom, while the east side represents fate. If there are more planets on one side than the other then this sways your reading.

LUNAR NODES

The lunar nodes are represented by the symbol ☊. These are the points at which the moon intercepts the sphere. Each astrology chart has a north and a south node, with the south node positioned directly opposite the north. Because the south node represents your past, who you have been, your instinctive behavior and your comfort zone, it doesn't tend to feature on birth charts, but is instead reserved for astrological readings later in life; the north node represents the opposite to the south node – where you should be heading in life, your aspirations and how you should challenge yourself to grow. The zodiac signs these two nodes fall into represent what these past and future characteristics should look like.

For example, on the birth chart on page 70, the north node falls into Leo, suggesting your future lies in surrounding yourself with others, rising to shine in your chosen field and being bold when making big decisions.

**THE STARRY VAULT
OF HEAVEN IS IN TRUTH
THE OPEN BOOK OF
COSMIC PROJECTION.**

CARL JUNG

How to discover your moon sign

Your moon sign refers to the astrological sign the Moon was travelling through at the time of your birth. The Moon takes two-and-a-half days to travel through each sign, so around one month to complete a cycle of all the signs of the zodiac.

Understanding your moon sign is important because it speaks of your emotional nature – your fears, longings, obsessions and everything in between. It is often called the "soul of your identity" – the subconscious part of you that remains hidden and perhaps you don't even know that well. Learning more about your moon sign can help to unlock these hidden traits and help you to understand yourself better.

Some call your moon sign your "inner child", your closely guarded emotional centre. It can have a big impact on your mood and the way your emotions make their way to the surface.

You will know your sun sign, but it's important to calculate your moon sign too in order to gain the bigger picture. You will feel incomplete without it.

How to calculate
your moon sign

In the past, in order to determine your moon
sign, you would have had to look up your time
and date of birth in a planetary ephemeris - an
extensive compendium of tables charting the Moon's
position throughout the days, months and years.
You can find your moon sign on your birth
chart. For example, on the birth chart on page
70, the moon sign falls into Sagittarius, suggesting
you are an independent soul and prefer to deal
with your emotions on your own.

You do not need to create your birth chart to
find out your moon sign, however. If you're after a
quick answer you can use an online calculator such
as lunarium.co.uk/calculators/moonsign. You will
need to know the exact time of your birth, as a few
minutes either way could push you to a different
sign entirely.

Understanding your moon sign

Aries – You are an impatient soul, powering through life at a stressful pace. It can be hard to plan ahead when all you think about is what is happening right now.

Taurus – You take things slowly and cautiously, remaining calm and paying attention to every detail. You are tactile and feel the need to keep people close.

Gemini – You thrive on learning and taking in new information – whether through interactions with others or reading books.

Cancer – Security is very important to you and there is a deep-rooted urge to also keep those around you safe.

Leo – You love being showered with praise and seek it wherever you can. You are keen to nurture your own talents and help others find theirs too.

Virgo – You are practical when it comes to taking care of yourself and others. Well-being is important to you and self-care high up on your priorities.

Libra – You love company and are drawn to people with whom you can create easy friendships. Well-being is high up on your agenda, particularly when it involves calm and peace.

Scorpio – You wear your emotions on your sleeve and can find it hard to hold back. Try a fast-paced workout if you need to shake off these feelings.

Sagittarius – You like your own space and the freedom to do things your way. You prefer to travel solo and deal with your emotions on your own.

Capricorn – You are a fan of routine – structure works for you and helps you to navigate day-to-day life as well as retain a feeling of control.

Aquarius – You don't follow the crowd and always want to explore alternative options. A sense of community is important to you as you seek like-minded folk.

Pisces – Your emotions can often confuse you – as can how to deal with those of other people. Often a little time out is the ideal solution.

What is a rising sign?

Your rising sign, also known as your "ascendant", is the constellation that was rising on the eastern horizon at the time of your birth – and it's just as important as your sun sign! As with your sun sign, there are 12 rising signs – from Aries to Pisces. While your sun sign reflects your personality, your rising sign reflects how you act.

For example, looking at the birth chart on page 70, if your sun sign is Pisces you might have a friendly, open personality and be incredibly creative, but with rising sign Capricorn you might act with stoicism and poise. (See pages 18–23 for an overview of the zodiac signs and traits.)

Your rising sign is associated with the first house of your chart (see page 85 for more about the houses), so it's all about new beginnings and self-identity. Your sun sign represents a bigger picture of you, while your rising sign represents the surface of your personality, a first impression if you will.

How to calculate your rising sign

These days we only need to search online to discover our rising sign, but in the past astrologers had to put pen to paper to work it out.

Your rising sign is very specific to the time of day you were born and is essential for an accurate birth chart. The rising sign changes frequently, so this information is key. If you've ever encountered a pushy astrologer who insisted you give up this information – this is why! With all 12 signs of the Zodiac rising in a 24-hour period, each takes a 2-hour window, which can then be connected to the time of your birth. If you are born at sunrise, your sun and rising signs will be the same.

Twins born 15 minutes apart could well have different rising signs, meaning their birth charts – and therefore their personalities – could differ greatly from each other.

While you can gather all of this information from your birth chart, if you are after a swift answer you can calculate your rising sign here: astrosofa.com/ascendant.

How to calculate your descendant

Your descendant is the sign that was setting on the western horizon at the time of your birth, it lies directly opposite your ascendant, in the seventh house, which represents relationships (see page 85 for more about the houses).

The descendant describes your desires, who you get along with and who you are attracted to.

It represents external obstacles that challenge you on a daily basis and what you desire but cannot reach.

Your descendant sign is important in understanding your behavior in relationships and reflects experiences that can help you to understand issues in a partnership.

For example, on the birth chart on page 70, the descendant is Cancer, suggesting you are attracted to people who make you feel emotionally secure and who you can be vulnerable with.

To discover your descendant, look at your birth chart or use the same link you used to calculate your ascendant and scroll down for your full astrological profile: astrosofa.com/ascendant.

Understanding the planets in your birth chart

With each planet reflecting a part of our psyche, there is much to be gained from a deeper understanding of their meaning. The planets indicate how we react to people and situations, and outline our dreams and desires. Don't worry if some of the houses on your birth chart do not contain any planets – this is quite common! Each planet has a sign that it naturally rules – a sign that it is often found frequenting. Use the information below when interpreting your birth chart and refer to page 17 for your sun-sign-specific guidance on the planets.

The Sun is our ego, will and determination, orbiting all the signs of the zodiac in the space of a calendar year.

The Moon reflects the part of ourselves that remains hidden, our memories and inner emotions. It transitions into a new sign every two-and-a-half days.

Mercury is the planet of communication, news and travel. It can also reflect gossip and rumor.

Venus is the planet of love, romance, sensuality and beauty. It helps us understand our love for others, but also things.

Mars is the planet of energy, action and conflict.

Saturn is the planet of commitment and stability. It also represents the restrictions placed on us.

Jupiter stands for spiritual growth and helps us to understand any emotional issues we may have.

Neptune is often referred to as "poetry of the soul", reflecting our deep-rooted emotions and creativity.

Uranus represents rebellion and the fight for injustice – in both our personal lives and on a global scale.

Pluto looks to change and how it can allow us to grow and achieve our dreams. This is the planet that forces us to face our fears and conquer them.

Understanding the houses in your birth chart

While your birth chart is divided into 12 sections that represent the sun signs of the zodiac, there are another 12 sections overlapping these called the "houses". Each house represents a different aspect of your everyday life, from your career, to travel, to love and more. Every planet on your chart is located in both a sun sign and a house, and their positions are key to deciphering your birth chart and understanding more about your inner workings. The houses are complex and far-reaching; the pages that follow offer a brief insight to get you started, but if you want to probe deeper refer to Resources on page 125 to find out even more.

FIRST HOUSE: PERSONALITY

This is the house of the self; it represents you, the body you were born with and your temperament. This is the house that symbolizes birth and new beginnings, reflecting how we view our life, and how our earliest encounters have impacted us and shaped our world. When planets move into this house, our goals are manifested and fresh new ideas begin to form.

Planets in this house

Sun – Self-development
Moon – Deep feelings
Mercury – Connection
Venus – Beauty
Mars – Strength
Jupiter – Optimism
Saturn – Foresight
Uranus – Individuality
Neptune – Glamour
Pluto – Control

Zodiac signs in this house

Aries – Motivation
Taurus – Balance
Gemini – Communication
Cancer – Protection
Leo – Action
Virgo – Order
Libra – Grace
Scorpio – Self-defense
Sagittarius – Vision
Capricorn – Planning
Aquarius – Clarity
Pisces – Imagination

SECOND HOUSE: POSSESSIONS AND MONEY

This house is all about material possessions and personal finances. It tells you about your attitude towards money – do you love it or hate it? It also gives you an insight into your personal finances – perhaps they are a source of concern, perhaps you're good at saving for a rainy day, or you could be rather frivolous – and how you earn it and spend it. Beyond finances, anything to do with worth and value can be found in this house – what we consider valuable in life and how we value ourselves.

Planets in this house

Sun – Independence
Moon – Security
Mercury – Communication
Venus – Sensuality
Mars – Ambition
Jupiter – Confidence
Saturn – Frugality
Uranus – Change
Neptune – Charity
Pluto – Survival

Zodiac signs in this house

Aries – Self-motivation
Taurus – Accumulation
Gemini – Light-heartedness
Cancer – Possessiveness
Leo – Pride
Virgo – Thriftiness
Libra – Equality
Scorpio – Privacy
Sagittarius – Frivolity
Capricorn – Planning
Aquarius – Sharing
Pisces – Generosity

THIRD HOUSE: COMMUNICATION

This house is all about how you communicate with those around you. How you express yourself and build relationships with others in your life – whether friends, family, co-workers, neighbors or those in the wider community – is at play here and when planets move into this house you can receive information about your network of associations. This house also has a strong focus on the language element of communication and also the relationships you have with your siblings.

Planets in this house

Sun – Language
Moon – Education
Mercury – Connection
Venus – Harmony
Mars – Competition
Jupiter – Optimism
Saturn – Authority
Uranus – Single-
    mindedness
Neptune – Intuition
Pluto – Learning

Zodiac signs in this house

Aries – Rivalry
Taurus – Learning
Gemini – Connection
Cancer – Protection
Leo – Confidence
Virgo – Organization
Libra – Equality
Scorpio – Education
Sagittarius – Adventure
Capricorn – Planning
Aquarius – Rationality
Pisces – Imagination

FOURTH HOUSE: HOME AND FAMILY

This house reflects your home, the place you regard as your safe haven or where your family resides. It's about where you feel a sense of belonging, sanctuary and security. The family in this house refers not just to your relations, but the family you choose for yourself through friends, neighbors and those in your local community. This house reflects your relationship with the maternal figure(s) in your life and looks to the situations in which you feel loved and looked after.

Planets in this house

Sun – Identity
Moon – Privacy
Mercury – Conversation
Venus – Peace
Mars – Conflict
Jupiter – Travel
Saturn – Stability
Uranus – Independence
Neptune – Sanctuary
Pluto – Renovation

Zodiac signs in this house

Aries – Rivalry
Taurus – Security
Gemini – Loyalty
Cancer – Protection
Leo – Pride
Virgo – Duty
Libra – Diplomacy
Scorpio – Privacy
Sagittarius – Welcome
Capricorn – Organization
Aquarius – Community
Pisces – Music

FIFTH HOUSE: CREATIVITY AND PLEASURE

As well as creativity and pleasure, this house is also linked with leisure, romance and those tiny bringers of joy, children, as well as our legacy. This house is all about what makes you feel good and brings you joy – whether that's getting your teeth into a creative project, feeling the rush of a confidence boost thanks to a compliment or career success, or the excitement of a new partner or life milestone. Risk-taking also falls into this house, so gamblers and extreme-sports enthusiasts take note.

Planets in this house
Sun – Attention
Moon – Playfulness
Mercury – Impulsivity
Venus – Communication
Mars – Competition
Jupiter – Fertility
Saturn – Strategy
Uranus – Originality
Neptune – Artistry
Pluto – Transformation

Zodiac signs in this house
Aries – Action
Taurus – Grounding
Gemini – Romantic connection
Cancer – Caretaking
Leo – Joyfulness
Virgo – Humility
Libra – Perfection
Scorpio – Loyalty
Sagittarius – Travel
Capricorn – Caution
Aquarius – Value
Pisces – Romance

SIXTH HOUSE: HEALTH AND WELL-BEING

As well as health and well-being, this house reflects your daily routines, which include jobs around the house and perhaps the more mundane tasks that you don't tend to give a second thought. Here is where to look for help in streamlining your schedules.

While the body you are born with is reflected in the first house, it is in this house that the focus lands on the body you have created over the course of your lifetime. Self-care, work–life balance, as well as mental and physical health are all covered here.

Planets in this house

Sun – Purpose
Moon – Hospitality
Mercury – Networking
Venus – Unity
Mars – Movement
Jupiter – Satisfaction
Saturn – Construction
Uranus – Change
Neptune – Music
Pluto – Nutrition

Zodiac signs in this house

Aries – Productivity
Taurus – Calm
Gemini – Dexterity
Cancer – Caretaking
Leo – Authority
Virgo – Detail
Libra – Diplomacy
Scorpio – Activity
Sagittarius – Freedom
Capricorn – Attention
Aquarius – Equality
Pisces – Structure

SEVENTH HOUSE: RELATIONSHIPS

Directly across from the first house, the seventh house reflects your life-changing relationships – not just romantic partners, but all significant relationships in your life. This house will look at negative as well as positive aspects of those relationships – offering potential insight into any disagreements you might have experienced among your nearest and dearest.

Planets in this house

Sun – Individuality
Moon – Sensitivity
Mercury – Knowledge
Venus – Value
Mars – Assertiveness
Jupiter – Motivation
Saturn – Commitment
Uranus – Independence
Neptune – Longing
Pluto – Transformation

Zodiac signs in this house

Aries – Equality
Taurus – Stability
Gemini – Variety
Cancer – Sentimentality
Leo – Desire
Virgo – Grounding
Libra – Compromise
Scorpio – Intensity
Sagittarius – Company
Capricorn – Security
Aquarius – Supportiveness
Pisces – Selflessness

EIGHTH HOUSE: SEX, DEATH AND TRANSFORMATION

This is the house in which we experience the darker aspects of life – emotional crises, loss and devastation – as well as the rituals, trials and tribulations of our existence. This house also reflects our intense romantic partnerships and adaptability to the ever-changing nature of our lives. This house teaches us that we need to embrace compromise in order to move forward, accept change and learn to derive power and inner strength from loss.

Planets in this house

Sun – Exploration
Moon – Intuition
Mercury – Secrecy
Venus – Diplomacy
Mars – Decisiveness
Jupiter – Positivity
Saturn – Boundaries
Uranus – Clarity
Neptune – Connection
Pluto – Power

Zodiac signs in this house

Aries – Impulsivity
Taurus – Investment
Gemini – Exploration
Cancer – Privacy
Leo – Financial success
Virgo – Catastrophe
Libra – Equality
Scorpio – Lust
Sagittarius – Risk-taking
Capricorn – Independence
Aquarius – Rationality
Pisces – Excitement

NINTH HOUSE: PHILOSOPHY AND ADVENTURE

This house looks ahead towards what we don't yet know – what lies beyond the horizon. Travel and higher education are also represented here – and those with birth charts showing planets in their ninth house are often extremely inquisitive and adventurous when it comes to travel. This house represents uncharted territory and curiosity – searching for a greater understanding of ourselves – as well as faith and politics.

Planets in this house
Sun – Confidence
Moon – Wanderlust
Mercury – Language
Venus – Creativity
Mars – Fearlessness
Jupiter – Teaching
Saturn – Caution
Uranus – Enlightenment
Neptune – Spirituality
Pluto – Education

Zodiac signs in this house
Aries – Independence
Taurus – Patience
Gemini – Curiosity
Cancer – Connection
Leo – Luxury
Virgo – Preparedness
Libra – Equality
Scorpio – Education
Sagittarius – Limitless
Capricorn – Ambition
Aquarius – Community
Pisces – Escape

TENTH HOUSE: CAREER

As well as your professional aspirations, this house also takes in social status and popularity. If you have planets in the tenth house on your birth chart you are no doubt an ambitious person when it comes to work life – and you know how to socialize with gusto. If you are feeling somewhat in limbo, this house may help to guide you towards your calling. Career changes are afoot when planets transition into this house.

Planets in this house	**Zodiac signs in this house**
Sun – Identity	Aries – Self-starter
Moon – Caring	Taurus – Loyalty
Mercury – Networking	Gemini – Variety
Venus – Diplomacy	Cancer – Nurturing
Mars – Competition	Leo – Self-promotion
Jupiter – Possibility	Virgo – Creativity
Saturn – Responsibility	Libra – Diplomacy
Uranus – Independence	Scorpio – Determination
Neptune – Creativity	Sagittarius – Achievement
Pluto – Influence	Capricorn – Organization
	Aquarius – Teamwork
	Pisces – Compassion

ELEVENTH HOUSE: FRIENDSHIP

This is the house that recognizes our social circle, and is where we find our place in the networks and groups in our lives. Here we find friendship, teamwork and common goals represented, as well as our support network, acquaintances and the way in which we spend time with those in our lives. Our social and political values come to the fore in this house, as does our ability to work with others to improve situations.

Planets in this house

Sun – Community
Moon – Extroversion
Mercury – Networking
Venus – Charm
Mars – Competition
Jupiter –
    Broadmindedness
Saturn – Commitment
Uranus – Freedom
Neptune – Self-sacrifice
Pluto – Empowerment

Zodiac signs in this house

Aries – Energy
Taurus – Constancy
Gemini – Diversity
Cancer – Safety
Leo – Leadership
Virgo – Caring
Libra – Harmony
Scorpio – Force
Sagittarius – Initiative
Capricorn – Control
Aquarius – Equality
Pisces – Sympathy

TWELFTH HOUSE: SACRIFICE

Sometimes known as the house of the unconscious, the twelfth house is also referred to as "the darkness before the dawn" – sitting just below the horizon, finishing off the houses before the cycle begins again. The "unconscious" speaks of all things without physical form, such as dreams, emotions and secrets. Planets take on an otherworldly quality in this house and this is where your good deeds are recognized.

Planets in this house

Sun – Purpose
Moon – Compassion
Mercury – Imagination
Venus – Self-reflection
Mars – Courage
Jupiter – Generosity
Saturn – Dedication
Uranus – Freedom
Neptune – Charity
Pluto – Acceptance

Zodiac signs in this house

Aries – Initiative
Taurus – Relaxation
Gemini – Ambition
Cancer – Caring
Leo – Creativity
Virgo – Thoughtfulness
Libra – Balance
Scorpio – Intuition
Sagittarius – Escape
Capricorn – Structure
Aquarius – Recharge
Pisces – Boundaries

Part 4
ASTROLOGY FOR SELF-CARE

We all need a little self-care in our lives and astrology can help steer you towards practices most suited to your sun sign and characteristics. As a Pisces, you are often thinking of others and whether they have everything they need. You can spend so much time looking after other people that you forget to look after yourself. Self-care for you involves some serious winding down – especially in the evening, to ensure your worrisome thoughts don't disrupt your sleep. Many Pisceans find their best self-care is regular yoga practice to keep their mind and body happy, while others look to journaling to relieve any tension. What helps you to de-stress? The following pages offer some ideas to help you find the methods best suited to you.

How to use astrology to guide self-care practices

By aligning your self-care practices with your sun sign, you can really boost their healing power. It's worth doing the research to get the most out of your downtime and rest. When it comes to yoga there are poses that offer a greater benefit to one sign over another, according to your personality and behaviors; and you will find favor in the crystals that match your sun sign, allowing energy to flow more freely with those assigned to you.

The following pages contain self-care rituals and practices specific to you and your sign. From tarot to crystals, the celestial body and your chakras, and de-stressing techniques, as well as the types of exercise that could suit you best.

As a Pisces, your focus is often on others – some might say this is a ploy to escape your own problems.

Whatever your reasoning, the burden of other people's problems can sometimes be hard to shake. Make room for some self-care in your life, remember that you need looking after too and take some time out to relax and improve your sleep.

You could try writing your thoughts and wishes in a journal or incorporating five to ten minutes of guided meditation into your day to banish any unhelpful thoughts.

Dos and don'ts

DO

+ Go at your own pace; self-care is not a race

+ What feels right; not every suggestion will be the one for you

+ Allow the guidance to help you to change bad habits

DON'T

+ Push yourself too hard; if you have a minor injury but the guidance is to do some strenuous exercise, give it a miss until you're feeling better

+ Give up things you love just because they're not mentioned as specific to your sign

+ Take risks if something doesn't feel right – stay safe and comfortable

**WE ARE MERELY THE
STARS' TENNIS-BALLS,
STRUCK AND BANDIED
WHICH WAY PLEASE THEM.**

JOHN WEBSTER

Rituals to help Pisces de-stress and unwind

We all have trouble sleeping sometimes, when life's stresses take over and our brain is left buzzing so much come bedtime that it disrupts our slumber.

A busy brain can be hard to quieten when there's been a lot going on during the day, so try heading to bed early for some restorative sleep and introduce a bedtime routine to really wind down. Spray lavender on your pillow and all around your bedroom, banish screens for at least an hour before bed and get comfortable with a good book or magazine.

If you need some help dropping off, investigate Calm, an app designed to help you de-stress and alleviate anxiety through guided meditation, sleep stories and soothing sounds. You'll likely find you don't reach the end of a sleep story as you are lulled into a deep slumber. Try the free version to see if it works for you before you sign up.

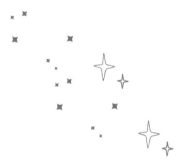

Writing in a journal before you go to bed can be a good step in a bedtime routine and help you banish unhelpful thoughts by writing them down before you go to sleep.

Try to scribble down three things you are grateful for before you go to sleep every night – these can be simple things that happened that day or bigger elements of your life. You'll find that the more you do this, the more positivity you bring into your life.

Yoga poses for Pisces

The benefits of yoga are far-reaching, from increasing flexibility, improving muscle strength and tone, boosting energy, promoting circulation and restorative sleep, to bringing you a sense of zen and relaxation.

The following yoga poses are ideal for you – you might also like to look into high-energy Bikram and flow styles of yoga, but remember to balance this with slow and thoughtful styles for maximum benefit.

Always make sure you warm up first and don't push your body. If you haven't tried yoga before, consider joining a class taught by an experienced yoga practitioner.

CHILD'S POSE

This simple and calming pose can be done at any time. If you find yourself restless in the middle of the night, try doing this pose on your bed to relax your body and get it ready to sleep again.

Kneel with your knees hip width apart and your toes touching each other. Exhale and fold yourself forward, resting your torso between your thighs.

Tuck your chin under and stretch your arms out on the mat in front of you. Let the weight of your shoulders open the shoulder blades and breathe. Rest here for from 30 seconds to a few minutes, whatever feels natural and needed.

TREE POSE

Stand with your feet together, shift your weight to one foot and spread out your toes. Slowly lift your other foot and place it on your inner thigh or on your calf – be careful not to press it to your knee. Bring your palms together in the center of your chest. If you wobble, focus on something – a spot on the floor perhaps – to help you keep your balance.

To take this pose further take your prayer hands and stretch them up above your head. Lift your chin and enjoy this stretch for several breaths. Then swap to the other side and perform the stretch again.

TRIANGLE POSE

This lengthening and strengthening pose is good for the thighs, torso, hips, groin, hamstrings, calves, shoulders and spine.

Stand on your mat with your feet together, shoulders back and your arms at your sides (this is known as mountain pose). Move your feet so they are about a yard apart. Stretch your arms out either side with palms down, parallel to the floor. Turn your right foot out by 90 degrees and your left foot in slightly. Turn your head to look over your right arm, to your fingertips. Strengthen your left leg and root your heel into the floor. Hinge at your hips to bring your right arm down to your ankle, if you can reach, and stretch your left arm upwards, fingertips reaching for the sky.

Hold this pose for a few breaths before swapping to the other side.

WARRIOR II POSE

This steadying pose will help you to build strength and stamina in your legs and ankles, as well as your shoulders, quads and core.

Stand with your feet about a yard apart. Turn your right foot out by 90 degrees and bring your left foot in slightly. Stretch your arms out on either side and bend your right knee so it is directly above your ankle. Sink your weight into your hips, turn your head to the right and hold, really feeling the deep stretch.

When you are ready, swap over to the other side.

**THERE IS NO BETTER
BOAT THAN A HOROSCOPE
TO HELP A MAN CROSS
OVER THE SEA OF LIFE.**

VARAHA MIHIRA

Exercise for Pisces

Water sign Pisces needs no excuse to go for a dip, so get out for a swim whenever you can – whether wild or in the pool – and feel your affinity with the cooling waves. For something a bit more high-energy you could investigate an aqua aerobics class or look into a swim challenge for something to work towards.

Try hatha or ashtanga yoga to really stretch out, focus on your breath and recharge. A regular meditation class could really do you good, too, and think about working on your core with Pilates.

If you find these more mindful activities are suited to you, why not think about attending a yoga retreat to really feel the benefit. There are dozens of options available, with varying lengths ranging from one day to a whole week, often also incorporating meditation and nourishing meals into the mix.

Try body-conditioning martial arts such as Taekwondo to build strength, stamina and patience. Using concise punching and kicking techniques alongside mental-strength training; this ancient martial art's history is rooted in self-defense, with mind and body participating in equal measure.

Crystals

Naturally occurring crystals contain piezoelectric and pyroelectric properties that cause them to vibrate. This, along with the fact that they are also conductors of heat and electricity, has led many to believe that they have the ability to transform your energy levels, help you find love and restore your health.

Crystals have been used in healing for thousands of years and evidence of this can be found in ancient texts. The vibrations are thought to help restore the body's natural healing mechanisms, as well as encouraging a sense of balance, calm and well-being. This type of practice is called "vibrational medicine".

People often select crystals according to their color as well as their properties, and their sun sign and birth date can come into play here too. Choosing crystals with your sun sign in mind can help to align you for a more successful experience. Bearing in mind the celestial body (see page 36) and matching crystals to the chakra related to your sun sign (see page 122) will also bring the most benefits.

Chakra	Location	Color	Emotional and physical associations
Root	Base of spine	Red	Feeling grounded, independent
Sacral	Just below navel	Orange	Acceptance, well-being, pleasure
Solar plexus	Base of ribcage	Yellow	Confidence, self-control, self-esteem
Heart	Centre of chest	Green	Love, joy, inner peace
Throat	Base of throat	Blue	Communication, self-expression
Third eye	Above and between brows	Indigo	Intuition, decision-making
Crown	Top of head	Violet	A feeling of connection, spirituality

CRYSTALS ACCORDING TO ZODIAC SIGN

Aries – Red jasper, carnelian, citrine

Taurus – Smoky quartz, amazonite, selenite

Gemini – Shungite, amazonite, tiger's eye

Cancer – Selenite, labradorite, red jasper

Leo – Tiger's eye, rose quartz, garnet

Virgo – Amazonite, amethyst, fluorite

Libra – Tiger's eye, amethyst, bloodstone

Scorpio – Pink tourmaline, amethyst, raindrop azurite

Sagittarius – Lepidolite, smoky quartz, shungite

Capricorn – Rose quartz, garnet, smoky quartz

Aquarius – Lepidolite, amethyst, tourmalinated quartz

Pisces – Clear quartz, carnelian, chrysocolla

CLEANSE YOUR CRYSTALS

Preparing your crystals before use is important in order to remove any negative or old energy. Rinse them under running water for a minute and leave to dry outside in the fresh air. Then submerge your crystals in salt water and leave out to air dry. Finally, leave your crystals to bathe in moonlight or sunlight for 12 hours. Now they are ready to use.

SELF-CARE WITH CRYSTALS

You might want to try using crystals to create a calming space in your home, or an area in which you want to nurture creativity. Follow these simple steps to shift energy and transform your safe space.

+ **Choose a quiet space in your home – perhaps an area of your living room or bedroom. Make sure this is a place where you can have a few moments away from any noise or other people, it is comfortable and you will be able to relax.**

+ **Allow air to flow through the space in order to rid it of any "dead energy". Then do some more physical dusting and clean it up, clearing away any dust or cobwebs, and decluttering so only a few things remain.**

+ **Add some crystals to bring a calm energy to the space – quartz and amethyst work well for this, promoting healing, cleansing and harmony.**

+ **Put the crystals in a place where they will catch the natural light, and make sure they each have some space and are not touching each other.**

Tarot

Tarot can be used for divination and anyone can do a reading – you don't need to visit a psychic or be one yourself to dabble with the deck. Either perform your reading yourself or ask a friend to do it and take it in turns. Tarot can offer insight and guidance by asking a question and interpreting cards pulled at random from the deck. Each of the 78 cards holds a unique meaning in relation to the question being asked.

The cards are made up of the major and minor arcana. The 22 major arcana cards feature some you might have heard of before, such as the Sun, the Moon, the Fool, Death and the Lovers. These represent karmic influences and themes in your life. If one of these appears in your reading, it often signifies the need to reflect on its life lessons. Each zodiac sign is ruled by a card from the major arcana. In the case of Pisces, the card is the Moon – which represents your ability to rely on your instincts and intuition.

The minor arcana features 56 cards grouped into four suits of 14 each; ten of these are numbered, along with a Page, Knight, Queen and King. These cards represent situations, guide you to make choices and reflect your state of mind.

Tarot itself is interpreted in different ways, with some believing the answers come from spirits or angels, while others favoring the explanation of synchronicity where the cards drawn are meaningfully related. If this is something that interests you, you're best to research tarot in more detail to understand the meanings behind each card, but the following pages will get you started with a few tips on how to set yourself up. With a little guidance, you can unlock the symbolism and begin a journey of self-discovery.

CHOOSING A DECK

It is supposedly bad luck to buy your first tarot deck yourself and believed that it should be given as a gift. However, this is often disregarded as archaic superstition, so if you're not bothered by that then go ahead and buy a deck yourself! It's important you have a good relationship with the deck of cards you end up using, so make sure you like the illustrations they feature. There are hundreds of different decks available, so do some research and choose some you like the look of. If you feel lost amid the variety, go for the ever-popular Rider-Waite-Smith deck.

ENERGIZING AND CLEANSING YOUR CARDS

A new deck needs to be energized, so once you've taken your cards out of their shiny wrapping be sure to give them a thorough shuffle. The best way to do this is to fan out the cards on a table and swirl them around until you're satisfied they're well and truly mixed up. Don't be precious, you want some of the cards to be upside down in order to give reversals in your readings, so swirl, mix and swirl again.

When you haven't used your deck for a while, it's a good idea to give it a cleanse to banish any negative energy. There are several ways you can do this: shuffle the deck and knock on it three times; place the cards on a window ledge overnight where they will be bathed in moonlight; burn some dried sage and pass the deck though the smoke a few times.

SETTING THE SCENE

In the beginning, it's a good idea to choose a space to practice where you will have some peace and quiet, and can give the deck your full attention. Choose a space that is calm and uncluttered – you want it to have a positive energy, so you could select a few items to help create the perfect space.

SETTING YOUR INTENTION

During a reading, it's vital you keep the positive energy flowing around you. An easy way to do this is to bathe the room in bright, white light – this will banish negative energy and keep it at bay for the duration of your reading.

READING AND QUESTIONING

Beginners are best off starting with a three-card spread, such as past, present and future. Make sure you have your question in your mind as you shuffle the deck. Cards that fly out of the deck while shuffling are symbolic. Deal three cards, face up, in front of you – past, present and future.

The more detailed the question you ask, the more detail you will have returned in your answer. Try to avoid vague questions or those that could have a simple "yes" or "no" answer. Think of questions that are more likely to open up a conversation. As a Pisces, you might want to ask detailed questions related to a creative project you are working on. Will you ever finish it? Ask the cards how it will all pan out.